WHAT
HAPPY COUPLES
Know

MARK FINLEY
AND
STEVEN MOSLEY

Pacific Press® Publishing Association
Nampa, Idaho
Oshawa, Ontario, Canada

Edited by B. Russell Holt
Designed by Tim Larson
Cover photo by Carol Kohen © Image Bank

Copyright © 2000 by
Pacific Press® Publishing Association
Printed in the United States of America

Unless otherwise noted, all Bible texts are from the New King James Version (NKJV), copyright © 1979, 1980, 1982 by Nelson, Inc., Publishers.

Scriptures quoted from NIV are from the Holy Bible, New International Version, copyright © 1973, 1978, 1984 by the International Bible Society. Used by permission of Zondervan Bible Publishers.

ISBN: 0-8163-1810-7

00 01 02 03 04 • 5 4 3 2 1

Contents

Introduction

This book is refreshingly different. You have read the divorce statistics. You have read horror stories about marriages falling apart, brokenhearted wives, and lonely children. Marriage is taking a hard hit these days. Even a casual view of television presents the home in deep trouble. Extramarital affairs, conflict in marriage, and families falling apart seem to be the norm.

What Happy Couples Know is different. It shares real-life stories of couples who have the ability to communicate, the ability to share their deepest feelings and listen sensitively to one another. There is a warmth, a love, a caring in their relationships.

In the first chapter, "We Talk It Out," these happy couples talk about the most important thing that keeps them together. They talk about a faith-based relationship with Jesus Christ that is not fake but genuine. These couples talk about the ability to share on the most intimate level.

In chapter two, "We Found a Best Friend," our happy couples talk about marriage as a friendship, a relationship, a bonding. They discuss marriage as a life commitment, not a tug of war or a one-upmanship or a competitive conflict.

These couples have gone through hard times, and the real-life couples that we interview in chapter three talk about "Trust Through the Hard Times." They talk about faith, about hanging on, about perseverance in their marriage, and the richness that comes from the love that Christ has given them in their hearts to trust in the difficult times.

Whether you are single or married, you will be enriched as you read *What Happy Couples Know* Its positive, cheerful, optimistic spirit will lift your own spirits. You will find renewed hope and courage as you read these pages. As you apply the practical principles outlined in this book, your own interpersonal relationships will improve. Those ragged edges on your marriage will be smoothed. Those bumps in the road will be leveled. If you are married, you will appreciate your own spouse much, much more. You will have a sense of a new love in your marriage, because there is a new love for Jesus in your own heart.

May your life be filled with the richness of His love as you read these pages.

Mark Finley and Steven Mosley

We Talk It Out

Happy couples. Sometimes you can spot them right away. They just have a look; they just have a way of being together. You know they've got it, and you wonder, "What's their secret; what makes them tick?"

In this chapter, we're going to find out.

They stand out in a time when couples are divorcing as often as they marry. They stand out in a time when some observers wonder if the family can really last long in the twenty-first century.

Happy couples stand out. They are people who just can't hide their joy in being together, people who've been together ten, twenty, thirty years, and still have a sparkle in their eyes.

They aren't likely to get prime time on television or in theaters. It's ugly divorces and wrenching affairs that dominate the story lines there. But in real life, these happy couples do give us pause; they make us wonder, "How do they do it? What is it that keeps them close over the years?"

Well, we decided to find out. So we talked to the happiest couples we could find. We talked to people who have been together through thick and thin and who are still enjoying the journey. And we asked them: "What's the most important thing that keeps you together? What keeps you close?"

Darlene Dickinson: "For us, the absolute top of the list is that we both have a personal relationship with Jesus Christ. You can fake it for a while, but the real thing has to be there. From the get-go we had that bond together."

Eldon Dickinson: "My faith and hers are lined up perfectly. Through the years it has deepened."

Jan Judd: "Both of us have a central focus of Christ in our life; we have the same goal of commitment to God. We've always prayed together as a family, and Warren and I still do. We talk a lot about God in our lives and our need of Him. When something makes us happy, we're open about talking about Jesus and our relationship with Him."

Warren Judd: "When you're focused on Christ as an example, it makes you more focused on being tolerant to a partner. You ask yourself, 'What would Jesus do?' "

Dan Savino: "I definitely think of my wife as a gift from God."

Val Savino: "We're committed to God. We both feel that God put us together and that this is what He has ordained, so we just go from there."

Mike Hanson: "We're both committed to the idea that the Lord's strength is a very real presence in our lives. We're committed Christians; we believe He will be there for us."

Sharon Hanson: "It's a wonderful security for me. Women love security. I've always known that this man loves God even more than me. It's a wonderful security for me because it affects how he treats me and the kids and his work. He's not perfect, but he has a heart for God, and he works on issues."

What keeps happy couples close through the years? The answer that we kept getting over and over was a very simple one—God. God is at the center of their marriages. Their commitment to Christ binds them together. In fact, in talking to them, you get a definite sense that their marriages take place *in* Christ's kingdom, that they have found a way inside that kingdom of grace.

Happy couples have found a way inside God's kingdom of grace. And it's not just that this commitment to God makes them joyful together. What's even more remarkable is when you find that same joy and closeness in the next generation.We are living in a time when divorce is what most kids inherit from their parents. It seems that dysfunction is the thing passed on from generation to generation. But these couples have created a far better legacy.

Mark Judd: "As a young couple making decisions about our future, we really have something to hang our decisions on because we have God and we both are committed to Him being the Leader. It brings us closer."

Andrea Judd: "When we haven't taken time for God, and our individual devotional life is not where we want it to be, we can tell the difference in our relationships overall. So we see the importance of taking time to connect with God together as a couple."

Happy couples don't just live together in a house; they live together in a certain kingdom, the kingdom of Christ.

In this book, we're going to focus on what that means and how that can affect our own relationships. We're going to discover that many of the principles of Christ's kingdom are great marriage principles, too. His teaching about the kingdom has a lot to say about the way a couple can bond together.

Let's focus on Christ's kingdom of grace. How did Jesus go about establishing His kingdom of grace? One word—forgiveness. Jesus went about sharing forgiveness with people who needed it—all kinds of people:

•" 'Take heart, son; your sins are forgiven' " (Mathew 9:2, NIV).
•" 'Go in peace and be freed from your suffering' "

(Mark 5:34, NIV).

• " 'The Son of Man has authority on earth to forgive sins' " (Mark 2:10, NIV).

• " 'Friend, your sins are forgiven' " (Luke 5:20, NIV).

These are the words Jesus spoke as He spread His kingdom through Galilee and Judea. His is a kingdom of grace. It's a kingdom of those who know they've been forgiven. And so, they learn to forgive.

Jesus once told a parable, recorded in Matthew 18, about a certain king who wanted to settle accounts with his servants. One owed a lot of money, the equivalent of millions of dollars today. But this man begged and pleaded for mercy. "Have patience, and I'll pay," he said.

The king was so moved with compassion that he simply canceled the debt, the whole thing!

What did this fortunate servant do as a result? He went out and found a fellow servant who owed him a few dollars. He grabbed him by the throat and said, "Pay me!"

This man begged for mercy, "Have patience, and I'll pay."

But the first servant refused; he had his debtor thrown in jail.

When the king found out about this, he called for his servant and said, " ' "You wicked servant! I forgave you all that debt because you begged me. Should you not also have had compassion on your fellow servant, just as I had pity on you?" ' " (Matthew 18:32, 33).

The point of this parable is that we human beings have been forgiven much. All those in Christ's kingdom have been forgiven a great deal. God has canceled our debt of sin, giving up His own Son. The offense of our transgression was wiped out at the Cross.

So what should we do when someone ruffles our feathers, slights us, offends us, doesn't take into account our feelings?

Should we brood over that little sin? Should we hold a grudge, use it as a weapon, try to make the other person pay?

No, we who have been shown such great compassion should show a little compassion as well. We who have been forgiven should forgive.

That's one of the most essential principles in Christ's kingdom of grace. God has been gracious to us, so we can be gracious to others.

And nowhere is that more important than in marriage! Happy couples have a strong sense that they've been forgiven much by God. That's why they can extend forgiveness more easily to their spouses. That's why they can cut each other a little slack, give each other a little space.

Ron Sorrels: "I think what's important is that each person, spiritually, have a God-centered relationship. You have to respect and allow that."

Darlene Dickinson: "With a commitment to Christ, you don't have to second-guess everything that happens. We turn our lives over to Him; then whatever happens today, you don't have recrimination—if I had only done this or that. If there's a problem, you take it as one of the lumps, instead of blaming the other person."

Mike Hanson: "Religion can be divisive if we make too great a priority of form over substance. The substance is always more important. It's our relationship with God that's kept us close. We have supported each other in that."

There's a wonderful verse that sums up this idea of the grace that pervades Christ's kingdom. Jesus said, " 'Do not fear, little flock, for it is your Father's good pleasure to give you the kingdom' " (Luke 12:32). God doesn't welcome people into the kingdom grudgingly. He is lavish in His grace. He is generous in His forgiveness. He has gladly chosen to give us the kingdom.

That's the kind of grace that couples who live *in* His kingdom of grace can extend to each other.

It has an impact on their marriage. It has an impact, above all, in the way they communicate. A sense of forgiveness, a sense of grace, makes it much easier to have open and honest communication. Couples aren't afraid that they are going to be dumped on for sharing their feelings. Couples don't have to keep things secret, to tiptoe around things no one can talk about.

Openness is another characteristic of Christ's kingdom of grace. Jesus once proclaimed this kingdom principle in these words: " 'For there is nothing covered that will not be revealed, and hidden that will not be known. Whatever I tell you in the dark, speak in the light; and what you hear in the ear, preach on the housetops' " (Matthew 10:26, 27).

That was Jesus' attitude. He wasn't afraid for His disciples to share what they'd seen and heard privately. He didn't try to keep things secret. He was confident that truth would win out in the light of day.

Couples who live in Christ's kingdom of grace benefit from this kind of open communication. In fact, they thrive on it.

Mark Judd: "It's great to have honest sharing, that constant openness and communication about everything."

Ron Todo: "One of the things I appreciate most is that I can discuss anything with my wife without fear of ridicule or being put down."

Kari Todo: "We can talk about anything and everything—and we do. In fact, someone will tell Ron something that I've said, but he knows I didn't say it because we talk about everything. Communication is the biggest thing in a marriage."

Mike Hanson: "There's no substitute for living life together and discovering things together. We've always been pretty good at talking about everything that happens. We've had deep conversations, not just surface talking. We really do get into each other's hearts and minds."

Ralph Figueroa: "One important thing is that we talk about everything that's on our minds so that nothing festers; it's not pent up. We talk about issues and problems right when they happen; they don't build up."

Happy couples talk it out. That's an essential component of marriages that last. And it's an essential component of marriages built on Christ's kingdom of grace.

But, happy couples don't just dump their feelings on each other; they don't just unload. There's also an element of kindness and consideration in how they communicate. Sharing your feelings doesn't mean you have to close out the feelings of your spouse.

Let me tell you about another kingdom principle that is vitally important to relationships, especially to marriages.

One evening, Jesus was being entertained at the home of a Pharisee. All the guests were offended when a sexually immoral woman sneaked in and began anointing Jesus' feet with perfume, as she wept. It was obviously a gesture of repentance and devotion. But everyone made indignant comments, humiliating the woman.

Jesus, however, spoke words in her defense. And His most powerful statement was this: " 'Therefore I say to you, her sins, which are many, are forgiven, for she loved much. But to whom little is forgiven, the same loves little' " (Luke 7:47).

What Jesus was saying to those indignant people was this: He who is forgiven much, loves much. You could learn from that.

This is another result of an awareness of grace, an awareness of how much God has forgiven us. We can love much. We can perform acts of kindness. We reach out to others with gracious gestures.

Couples who live in Christ's kingdom of grace communicate openly, but they communicate with kindness.

Sharon Hanson: "We've always been polite to each other. That's a habit you develop. It doesn't mean we're surface, but we try not to interrupt when the other is talking, even saying hurtful things. You do share your feelings, but there are ways to share them without being rude to each other."

Ron Todo: "We've learned that fighting is OK, but we have to respect each other's boundaries. Sometimes we have to say, 'OK, this needs to stop,' and we'll come back to it when we're more rational and work it out."

Ralph Figueroa: "After I got married, I realized that I had an attention problem. Often when

Heidi speaks, I don't catch the first words; she has to repeat herself. But she didn't trash me about that. She's been very patient and worked with me."

Heidi Figueroa: "Just being gracious and saying 'thank you' is important for us. Many times life is mundane; routine things go unnoticed. But we try to notice good things—saying how good a meal was or expressing appreciation for help around the house."

Happy couples communicate with kindness because they are living in a kingdom of grace.

The principles of Christ's kingdom can indeed make a huge difference in our marriages. I have learned this over the years with my wife, Teenie. I have learned that our bond in Christ is one of the strongest bonds two people can have.

In His Sermon on the Mount, Christ gives us another kingdom principle that relates wonderfully to marriage. It really sums up what these happy couples we've been quoting have in common. " 'But seek first the kingdom of God and His righteousness, and all these things shall be added to you' " (Matthew 6:33).

Christ was pointing out, first of all, that our basic needs for food and clothing would be taken care of—if we seek God first. But this principle has special meaning for couples. Those committed to the kingdom of God *do* find that "all these things" that they need fall into place. The things that bind a couple together are "added to" them. That's what living in the kingdom of grace does.

- •Couples who realize how much they have been forgiven can be more forgiving.
- •Couples who have received grace can be more gracious.
- •They can communicate more openly.
- •They can communicate with kindness.

He who has been forgiven much, loves much. That's a great principle of the kingdom of grace. It's a great principle of marriage. It's what makes happy couples tick. When they look back on their years together, it's the little acts of kindness that stick in their minds.

Dan Savino: "I think the single most precious moment in our marriage came late on a Friday afternoon. I told Val I was going out to the market. She said, 'Can I come?' I said, 'Sure.' After we got in the car, she asked, 'What do you have to pick up?' Well, I'd planned it to be a bit more of a surprise. But I had to admit to her that I was going to pick up the flowers I get her every week. 'You don't have to do that,' she said, but, of course, she appreciated it. And then I asked her, 'And what do you need to pick up?' 'Oh nothing,' she said, 'I just wanted to be with you.' Well, it hit me. We've been married twenty-seven years, and still—I was on an errand for her, and she was saying she loved to be with me. 'I'm here just because I want to be with you.' That felt about as warm as it gets!"

Happy couples happen because Christ's kingdom of grace happens. Happy couples stay happy through the years because Christ's forgiveness and grace stay real for them.

Wouldn't you like to step into that kingdom? Wouldn't you like to base your life and your marriage on the forgiveness that God so graciously offers?

You can join the couples who've really got it, the couples who are happily bonded together. Learn more of their secrets in the next chapter.

We Found a Best Friend

Jan Judd: "He's just always lovely to me; what can I say?"

Mike Hanson: "Sharon has great insight into people's personalities. And she's almost always a positive, joyful person."

Mark Judd: "One thing I'm so thankful for is that I have a wife who is committed to living in the center of God's will for our lives. There's never a tug of war, with one of us wanting God's will more than the other. I have a soul mate who's committed to God's will."

Myrna Sorrels: "I most appreciate his honesty; he's very supportive."

Andrea Judd: "Mark is a great spiritual leader in our home."

Eldon Dickinson: "She's a perfect person of her word. It's one of her wonderful traits."

Warren Judd: "There's a level of innocence in Jan, a vulnerability, that's refreshing; I appreciate that."

Have you noticed that some couples, couples who've been married many years, don't just love each other, they *like* each other? They still think they're married to a wonderful person. Are they just incredibly lucky? Or do they understand something that everyone needs to know?

Dan Savino: "I think that when each person in a marriage believes that he or she got the best end of the deal, that's ideal. I've never doubted that I'm far luckier in having Val as my wife than she is in having me as her husband."

Val Savino: "I am just in awe that God put me with this man, and I'm truly grateful. So how can our marriage not work?"

Isn't that a beautiful attitude to have? Couples like this seem to have stumbled on one of the great secrets of happiness in a relationship: somehow, they remain likable, and they remain appreciative and grateful.

How exactly does this happen? In this book, we're trying to find answers by talking with happy couples, couples who've remained happy through the years. And one thing we've discovered is that these couples base their relationships on a commitment to God. They build their relationships in Christ's kingdom. The principles of Christ mold their marriages.

In this chapter, we're going to talk about a certain characteristic of Christ's kingdom that helps people to *like* each other, as well as love each other. It's a principle that helps keep them thankful. Yes, believe it or not, there are many couples who are thankful that they have found, in their spouse, a best friend.

Ron Todo: "The best thing in marriage is having a best friend whom I can always count on. She knows me better than anyone else ever has known me or does know me."

Sharon Hanson: "We were best friends before we became lovers."

Mike Hanson: "I think one of the best things about our marriage is that we have always been good friends. We were good friends before we fell in love and have continued that friendship along with our marriage through the years. I tend to think of her as my best friend and confidant; she's my greatest cheerleader, and I am hers. We really like each other."

Myrna Sorrels: "We've always been best friends. Even when we had disagreements, we cared that the other understood where we were coming from. We just enjoy each other."

Mike Hanson: "There's a spiritual oneness about us that, I think, is God's gift. We feel we're an answer to each other's prayers, that we've found our soul mates."

Let's look at this spiritual oneness these happy couples feel is God's gift to them. Let's look at its roots in the kingdom of Christ.

One aspect of Christ's kingdom that seems to have affected these happy couples greatly is this: Christ's kingdom is a kingdom of *blessing!*

- Christ blessed people everywhere He went.
- He blessed lepers and publicans and prostitutes.
- He blessed the lame and the blind.
- He blessed a tax collector up in a tree.
- He blessed the poor in spirit and those who mourn.
- He blessed little children when the disciples were trying to usher them away.
- He blessed the multitudes.
- He blessed a thief crucified beside Him.

The apostle John summed it up in this way: "From the fullness of his grace we have all received one blessing after another" (John 1:16, NIV). One blessing after another—that's what happens in Christ's kingdom. It's a kingdom of blessing. And what we've discovered, after talking to happy couples, is that they've managed to tap into this kingdom of blessing, this attitude of blessing.

Mike Hanson: "Together, we hold things to be true that we believe come from God's Word. We're both committed to the idea that God wants good for His people, that He wants them to have happy lives. That He gives hopes and dreams and visions. That He's a force for potentiality. We think it's true on a practical level. All the things we can hope for are essentially possible. There are not a lot of limitations except the ones we put on ourselves. So we share that common philosophy. It's come about over time."

Happy couples are not just looking out for their own needs. They're not just trying to protect their own turf. They are convinced that they can each bless the other. They are convinced that each can help the other blossom. And that attitude starts with seeing your partner as a separate human being, someone with his or her own needs and abilities. It's the opposite of having to control, of trying to mold your partner in your own image.

Myrna Sorrels: "I think it's important to let each person be himself instead of trying to change him. I come from a stronger Christian background than Ron does. He hadn't seen a husband-wife situation that worked out. God was very much a part of my background, and knowing how God accepted me helped me accept Ron. His faith has grown because of that. I've allowed him to grow at his pace."

Ron Sorrels: "In our situation, Myrna had a stronger Christian background than me. My family was not as strong. So in the beginning our expectations were different. She was much more interested in church. It was difficult. But she let my interest grow. I can say from experience that if Myrna had tried to twist my arm, I wouldn't have found as much happiness and commitment to the church as I do today. Once we came to the conclusion we had to give each other space, to love each other the way we were and not box each other according to what we expected, things smoothed out a lot. When you first get married, you have preconceived notions. Once we got past that, our marriage smoothed out dramatically. The critical thing in our relationship is not to try to live the other person's life or idealize it; we accept each other for who we are."

Darlene Dickinson: "I'm a strong, independent type; so is Eldon. We would never tell each other to do or not do something. Each of us always has a choice. I wasn't thrilled about Eldon bungee jumping, but it was something he really wanted to do. You have to allow the other person to be in control of his or her life. God was willing to die to give us freedom of choice. But once you have that freedom, then you do consult each other about a lot of things."

Mike Hanson: "A good friend is someone in whom you see potential. You're willing to invest yourself in helping him reach that potential and possibility. I really think we are to be 'completers' of each other and not 'competors.' I've been my wife's biggest fan on any musical projects. When a few years ago she began to show God's calling in terms of speaking, I encouraged her to pursue that."

These are people who are living in Christ's kingdom of blessing. They are thinking about how they can bless each other.

So many couples get caught up in little rivalries, tugs of war. They're competing in subtle ways. Christ's disciples got caught up in that on more than one occasion. Walking along the road one day, they fell into an argument over who was greatest in the kingdom of heaven. It started out as an abstract discussion, but soon it involved jealousy and rivalry.

Jesus stopped them. He had something to say. It's recorded in Mark. " 'If anyone desires to be first, he shall be last of all and servant of all' " (Mark 9:35). And then Jesus took a little child in His arms and said, " 'Whoever receives one of these little children in My name receives Me' " (verse 37). How do you become great in Christ's kingdom, Christ's kingdom of blessing? You become a servant. You care for the weakest. You nurture the most vulnerable.

This is what happy couples have learned. They don't lose their identity in marriage. They don't lose their rights. But they do stop competing. There's plenty of blessing to go around. They concentrate on how they can bless their partner.

In Luke 18, we find another kingdom principle that relates wonderfully to marriage. " 'Everyone who exalts himself will be humbled, and he who humbles himself will be exalted' " (Luke 18:14).

Trying hard to end up on top, trying hard to dominate in a relationship, always puts us on the bottom. We destroy intimacy. We break down nurture. People who are genuinely humble just aren't worried about their relative position. They're not self-absorbed. They move out of themselves to bless other people. And the secret of genuine humility is to stay in Christ's kingdom of blessing. When you know that you've been blessed, you naturally become more humble, more grateful, more appreciative.

Happy couples are not rivals. They concentrate on blessing each other.

And here's another thing we discovered about the happiest couples. It relates to the way they see differences. Happy couples have the same differences that everyone else does. They have opposite temperaments. Their personalities sometimes clash. But over time they have learned to do something very important. They have learned to see opposite qualities in their partners as something *that they themselves need!* They have learned to see differences as a *blessing!* They are two different people who really complete each other.

Myrna Sorrels: "Ron has a more adventurous spirit than I do; I'm more cautious. But it's been good; I've tried things I wouldn't have otherwise."

Ron Todo: "I have someone to share the joy and excitement that I don't always show other people.

My wife definitely brings things out of me that others don't. I'm a pretty private individual; she gets inside of my personal life and brings things out."

Kari Todo: "Yes, we balance each other big time. I'm the talker; Ron's quiet. I'm outgoing and intense; he's laid back. We're complementary; we're more of a whole piece when we're together."

Dan Savino: "From my perspective, Val simplifies my life and does those things that I wouldn't without her. I'm cared for. She makes sure I'm getting what I need, and sometimes more. She is more disciplined in some areas. I would say Val is more disciplined spiritually. She doesn't allow me to take my spiritual life for granted."

Ron Sorrels: "Our personalities are so different. Myrna's a balance for me; she gives me balance. She never quits, never gives up, where I might be more inclined to throw up my hands. She's very methodical."

Warren Judd: "We balance each other out. We're almost opposite in many ways. My wife's into details, whereas I'm a big-picture person. She's a worrier; I'm an eternal optimist. But it works. When it comes to details, she makes very sure we take care of those. I would let a lot of that slip. It's good to have someone caring for details. I need to be tolerant of that because the details do make a difference in the long term. I don't mind at all trying to keep her focused on the big picture, bigger perspective. I like to fix broken things; I'm a practical person. Jan's not. I enjoy the fact that I'm called upon to make things work. I feel needed."

Couples who live in Christ's kingdom of blessing learn how to bless, and they learn how to be blessed. They learn how to benefit from the opposite qualities of the other person.

That's something that Jesus had to teach some of His closest friends. One day He was visiting in the home of Mary and Martha. It had become a place of refuge and rest for Him.

Mary and Martha were sisters with pretty opposite temperaments. Mary was the introspective dreamer, the thinker who thrived on deep relationships. Martha was more the driven, busy bee, always flitting from one chore to the other, always trying to get things done.

On one occasion, Martha was bustling around the house trying to get a big dinner ready and served to Jesus and His disciples. Mary was just sitting there, enraptured by Jesus' every word.

Martha began getting more and more annoyed. Couldn't her sister see how busy she was? Finally, she blurted out, " 'Lord, do You not care that my sister has left me to serve alone? Therefore tell her to help me' " (Luke 10:40). Martha wanted her sister to be more like her. She was sure Mary needed to be more like her.

But Jesus told Martha something else. " 'Martha, Martha, you are worried and troubled about many things. But one thing is needed, and Mary has chosen that good part, which will not be taken away from her' " (verses 41, 42).

Jesus wanted Martha to realize she needed to be more like Mary—rather than Mary becoming more like her. In her rushing about the house, in her need to impress everyone with what a perfect hostess she was, Martha had forgotten the one most important thing—enjoying her guests. She had forgotten that sometimes it's good just to sit and listen. Sometimes it's good to be like Mary.

- Learn from each other. Don't judge each other.
- Take the log out of your own eye. Don't try to get the speck out of the other person's eye.

Those are kingdom principles. They are principles of Christ's kingdom of blessing that relate powerfully to marriage.

Jesus wanted His followers to be the salt of the earth and the light of the world. He wanted His followers to spread His blessings. That's what couples can do for each other, too.

- Each person can free the other to be himself, to find his potential.
- Each person can balance and complete the other.
- That can happen as two people grow in the kingdom of blessing.

Christ once issued this wonderful invitation: " 'Come to Me, all you who labor and are heavy laden, and I will give you rest. Take My yoke upon you and learn from Me, for I am gentle and lowly in heart, and you will find rest for your souls. For My yoke is easy and My burden is light' " (Matthew 11:28-30).

Christ's yoke of discipleship is easy and light. It's a relief for those who are burdened. Why? Because Christ always wants to bless us; He always works for our good.

Remember that Christ's relationship with His disciples, with His church, is described as a model for the relationship of husband with wife. The bond of marriage should never be a heavy yoke; it should never be a burden. One person should never be molded into the image of the other. One person should never be controlled by the other.

The bond of marriage should be easy and light. It should be a commitment of individuals who are gentle and lowly in heart toward each other, and that happens when both are firmly planted in Christ's kingdom of blessing. That happens when two people are seeking to bless each other, instead of control each other. The result is something wonderful. It's two married people who remain two best friends.

Mike Hanson: "Sharon is the most fascinating person on the earth to me, and I want to know what she's thinking, how she's coping with experiences. We've lived a lot of our lives together. I'd do anything to be able to spend more time with her. When I think of fun things to do, they're usually not something to do by myself; they involve Sharon. We do well by ourselves; we're competent, capable people. But our choice is that, if we can, we'd rather be together. It's a wonderful thing to have."

Are you working to fulfill your spouse's dreams? Or are you trying to lock him or her into your own desires? Are you dedicated to helping your spouse become more complete as a person? Or are you trying to make him or her just like you?

You can find a best friend in your marriage, if you plant your feet in Christ's kingdom of blessing. You can find happiness, if you both seek the happiness of the other. Why not make a commitment to do that?

We Trust Through the Hard Times

It happens in every marriage. The tough times. The heartache. Sometimes it brings people together; sometimes it pushes them apart. Today, we'll discover what makes the difference.

Maybe it's a financial crisis—someone loses a job or falls into debt. Maybe it's a health problem—someone requires extensive surgery or is debilitated. Maybe it's a problem involving the children. But sometime, somewhere, most marriages run into hard times. The extended honeymoon turns into the school of hard knocks. The momentum of having fun together runs into some immovable object.

Many couples have a difficult time staying together through those tough times. Their relationship is strained and frayed. Sometimes it doesn't survive. And yet, other couples survive quite well. They even seem to thrive amid difficulty. The crisis makes them closer.

To find out what makes the difference we decided to talk to happy couples, couples who've stuck together through the ups and downs over the years. We wanted to hear about what has kept them close. And the first thing we learned was that these people didn't go through the tough times by themselves.

Mike Hanson: "We both believe that God is there in our times of trouble. That has been a great help. We didn't always see how that would be manifested. But it has. We faced the crisis early on, and we were just determined, with God's help, to work through things together."

Sharon Hanson: "It was tough losing our daughter. But these are things you have to work through. Mike mourned differently than I did, but we both knew that God was there with us through it all."

Val Savino: "I was extremely close to my grandmother. When she died, it drew Dan and me closer. We just had to get through it. And we knew God understood. I was telling God, 'I can't pray, but I love You. I know You're there. Just remember all the prayers from years before.' And then you remember that you love each other, too, and that you'll get through this."

Dan Savino: "In tough times you do feel that God holds you up."

Ralph Figueroa: "The fact that we both have

similar, fundamental beliefs is critical. It really smoothes things out for us in the tough times. We know that we're both in God's hands."

Heidi Figueroa: "It helps to be able to express your faith in God during the hard times, to be with someone who shares that same faith."

Mark Judd: "When things don't seem to be smooth, it helps that we're both convinced we live by God's assignments. When conflicts come, we can really sit down and examine—not necessarily 'How do we fix this?' but 'What's God saying to us right now, in this situation?' He's not necessarily causing the tough time, but we are in it, and He's led us so far. What is He saying to us right now? We can learn something from it."

Andrea Judd: "The main thing is not to ignore the difficulty and hope it will go away. Mark makes a point to sit me down and talk about the problem and pray about it. We take it to God."

Yes, there are couples who stay close through the hard times. There are couples who use adversity to grow. And they tend to be people who don't go through it alone. They believe, in fact, that God is on their side through all of it.

Couples who stay close through thick and thin are people who are firmly grounded in the kingdom of Christ. And they tap into a certain aspect of Christ's kingdom, something that gives them resilience, that gives them stability in a crisis. For them, Christ's kingdom is the kingdom of the chosen. That's what they experience—God choosing them.

Do you know the one thing Jesus emphasized as He went about establishing His kingdom? He emphasized a kingdom of the chosen.

- " 'I know whom I have chosen' " (John 13:18).
- " 'I chose you out of the world' " (John 15:19).

In His final discourse to His disciples, Jesus made the point very clear. He told this group that He could now call them "friends," not just "servants." And he said this: " 'You did not choose Me, but I chose you and appointed you that you should go and bear fruit, and that your fruit should remain, that whatever you ask the Father in My name He may give you' " (John 15:16).

Christ's kingdom is based on His choosing, His gracious choosing of us. He wants us to bear fruit, to be established, to have direct access to the Father.

Couples who stick together through adversity have this sense of being chosen, being part of Christ's kingdom of the chosen. What that means in practical terms is that God has a plan for them. He has a plan even in the worst of times. And that makes a big difference.

Ron Todo: "We have a belief that we can make

it through tough times. God is part of that process. E.W. Tozer makes a statement that the two of us together, with God, can become something far greater than just the two of us alone. And I've seen how that works in our marriage. God is with us and holding us accountable."

Kari Todo: "We do have faith that we will get through hard times, and we've been through them. There's an overall plan for our marriage, our family, our lives. Focusing on that fact, focusing on prayer, and believing that eventually God is going to show us that plan has been important."

Sharon Hanson: "In hard times we find that we can work together toward the same goals. There was a time when our major goal was to keep our daughter alive. We were working together toward a goal. We were both aiming toward that. We didn't live separate lives. And we believed that we were working with God toward what He wanted for us."

Eldon Dickinson: "I think when people hit a pothole, some clench their fists and say, 'Why me?' But somehow when we've come out on the other side, we've come out stronger. I credit the Lord for that. He strengthens us. When I had brain surgery in 1981, it was tough. But I remember a statement that goes like this: 'Behind the play and counterplay, it's God working out His purposes.' That has become our family motto. We're going to trust Him through those times."

God has a plan. That's a bedrock belief among couples who thrive in difficult times. And it's a part of Christ's kingdom of the chosen. Think, for example, of just how Jesus chose Simon Peter.

Peter had been out fishing all night with nothing to show for it. He was washing out his nets in the morning when Jesus, followed by a large crowd, walked up and got into his boat. Jesus spoke to the multitude for a while, then asked Peter to put out from the shore toward the deep waters.

And He told him to drop his nets for a catch.

Well, Peter knew perfectly well that no one caught fish at this hour. But he threw out his nets anyway.

And quickly, they filled with an enormous catch.

Peter was so awed by this, he said, " 'Depart from me, for I am a sinful man, O Lord!' " (Luke 5:8).

But Jesus replied: " 'Do not be afraid. From now on you will catch men' " (verse 10).

As soon as Peter landed his boat, Luke tells us, he left everything behind and followed Christ. Why did Peter, a successful, established fisherman, take that radical step? Because the One who chose him demonstrated that He had a plan. He could take care of things. He could provide. He knew more about fishing than Peter did, who'd spent his life on the Sea of Galilee.

" 'Follow Me,' " Jesus said, " 'and I will make you fishers of men' " (see Mark 1:17). Peter and the other disciples answered that call and walked into the kingdom of the chosen. They did so because they saw that Jesus had a plan. And no matter what challenges they might face, no matter what trials they might go through, they believed He could work all things for their good.

Couples who stand fast in the hard times have answered that call, "Follow Me." They have walked into the kingdom of the chosen. They've become part of God's wonderful plan.

There's another thing that characterizes couples who live out their marriages in Christ's kingdom. Because they have a strong sense of being chosen, they can choose too; they can make firm commitments. God went through a great deal in order to create His kingdom for the chosen in this sinful world. He made the ultimate sacrifice, giving up His one and only Son to rescue us, to choose us as His own.

Couples who understand that are capable of choosing each other, for better or for worse. They are willing to make sacrifices; they are willing to go the extra mile.

Warren Judd: "One thing that gets us through hard times is simply that separation is not an option. I'm committed to the long term in this deal, I'm not looking for an easy way out. It's not that I'm merely tolerating a poor situation. I enjoy living with Jan immensely. We're best friends as well as being husband and wife and lovers. But checking out when it gets rough is not an option for me."

Jan Judd: "If you're in the wrong, it helps to be willing to say you're sorry and not hang on to your hurt. Swallow your pride and work to restore the relationship. It's amazing what happens when you're willing to do that."

Mark Judd: "Each of us has a stability and security knowing that the other sees our relationship as a covenant and not just something based on—'I hope we'll still feel the same in ten years.'"

Ron Sorrels: "Today, there's a tendency to say, 'I'm not happy; this isn't what I had in mind. I'm out of here.' There's less of a desire to make things work. I think what keeps us strong goes back to the New Testament principle—'Wives, love your husbands. Husbands, love your wives.' That's a real commitment."

Sharon Hanson: "We have a history. We have a life together. When our daughter was diagnosed, and they said that 90 percent of husbands and wives who deal with terminal illness get divorced—well, I dug my heels in; it wasn't going to happen to us. It was hard. Caring for my daughter sometimes took up all my time and energy. But Mike loved her, too. There are times when you just have to deal with what you have."

Mike Hanson: "When we dealt with this crisis, I think the promises we'd made to each other were still fresh in our minds. We were in this for better or for worse. The worse was a life-threatening illness for our child. I think we were both committed to do whatever we could to experience a *quality* of family life even if we didn't have a *quantity*. We were very much in love, and we wanted to do the best for our kids. We were going to face the problems together."

Sharon Hanson: "Going out the back door was never an option. When you take that option off the table, there's nothing else to do but to work through it. It was a decision. There are valleys when you wonder. But you wait, you pass it, and the mountains come again. You have to get mature enough to realize that the grass is never greener somewhere else. We both want to stay married. If you want something bad enough, you'll change; that's the bottom line. So we grew together. You both have to want something so badly that you both are willing to change."

Couples who thrive in hard times have made a deliberate choice, a deliberate commitment. They are part of Christ's kingdom of the chosen, and they choose each other completely.

A wealthy young man once came up to Jesus with an important question: "What should I do to gain eternal life?"

Jesus asked him about his adherence to the Ten Commandments.

The man replied that he'd kept the law faithfully since he was a boy. And he asked, "What do I still lack?"

Jesus looked into this young man's eyes and felt a love for him. But He realized there was something holding him back. He had an unhealthy attachment to his wealth. His possessions were creating a barrier to his relationship with God.

So Jesus told him, " 'If you want to be perfect, go, sell what you have and give to the poor, and you will have treasure in heaven; and come, follow Me' " (Matthew 19:21).

This seems like a very difficult command. But Jesus knew what this young man needed to do in order to truly follow Him, in order to truly choose. Something was holding him back, and he needed to let go of it.

That's an essential part of coming into the kingdom of the chosen. You can't choose half-heartedly. You can't serve both God and money, for example. You have to forsake all other things that interfere with that primary allegiance.

Couples who stick close through the hard times feel this kind of commitment. They don't choose half-heartedly. They have forsaken all others. They don't hold on to anything that would interfere with their marriage commitment.

These happy couples have made a decision to walk together in Christ's kingdom of the chosen. And as a result, they find something wonderful. They discover the joy of having someone who's always there for them.

Dan Savino: "It's great to have someone you believe is true-blue. A year and a half ago, I had to go get a physical. They misdiagnosed my chest X-ray and noticed a mass in my chest. The doctor said, 'You're not going anywhere but the hospital.' I'll never forget what Val said as soon as she heard about this: 'I want you to know I'm with you all the way.' That's the kind of commitment you say at the altar, but thirty years down the line it's wonderful to know someone is there with you, right to the end.

"And it was a privilege for me to be there for her when she lost her dear grandmother. You just have to be there and help talk and cry things out together. But you know, I've discovered that I can't out-cry Val. She always feels what I'm going through; she feels it even more than I do."

Val Savino: "I think Dan has been there for me most of all in helping me learn to communicate. It was hard for me during those first years. I came from a family that could go for days without talking. It was pretty dysfunctional. Dan came from an Italian family in which everyone talks at once and everyone understands. I hadn't learned to trust. When I'd get mad, I'd just bottle it up. But Dan worked with me. He dragged it out of me and helped me to talk things out. I'm so glad he helped me learn to do that."

Mark Judd: "One thing that's great is that we're both seeking God in our decision making. We're there together trying to discover God's will. So if something goes wrong, it's not something one of us has to feel bad for, no matter who pushed for it. We hang it all on God; we don't have to blame each other. We're in this journey together."

Jan Judd: "I remember how, in all the things I tried to do as a mother, Warren stood by me 100 percent. That has meant a lot. We're in it together."

Eldon Dickinson: "Darlene has proved herself to be utterly trustworthy over the years, very fair and trustworthy. That has meant a lot."

Sharon Hanson: "Mike's always done things to show me that I'm the number one person in his life. That gives me great security."

Mike Hanson: "Sharon has been such a valuable resource for me in my work. I've benefited from her insights so much."

Myrna Sorrels: "I've always appreciated Ron's honesty, and he's always been very supportive."

Having someone who'll always be there for you—who could put a price tag on that? Who wouldn't want to forsake all others for that?

There is great benefit in building your relationships, your marriage, in Christ's kingdom of the chosen. There is great benefit in really understanding that God has chosen you. That He has gone to great lengths to choose you. You will realize that He has a plan, a wonderful plan for your life—both in good times and bad. You will be able to make a stronger commitment. You will be able to grow closer to your spouse when things get rough.

Wouldn't you like to have that kind of bond as a couple? You can take the essential steps to get there right now. You can take steps to start again—in the kingdom of the chosen. Won't you please make that commitment now—to God and to each other?

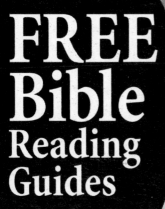
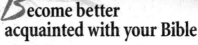